# A Pocket Full of Hope

## FOR WHEN YOUR POCKET IS EMPTY

*Don't lose your HOPE!*

Ayesha O. Daniels

ISBN 978-1-0980-9566-6 (paperback)
ISBN 978-1-0980-9567-3 (digital)

Copyright © 2021 by Ayesha O. Daniels

All rights reserved. No part of this publication may be reproduced, distributed, or transmitted in any form or by any means, including photocopying, recording, or other electronic or mechanical methods without the prior written permission of the publisher. For permission requests, solicit the publisher via the address below.

Christian Faith Publishing, Inc.
832 Park Avenue
Meadville, PA 16335
www.christianfaithpublishing.com

Unless otherwise noted, Scripture quotations are taken from the NEW AMERICAN STANDARD BIBLE ®, Copyright © 1960, 1962, 1963, 1968, 1971, 1972, 1973, 1975, 1977, 1995 by The Lockman Foundation. Used by permission.

Printed in the United States of America

To my loving father, Joseph G. Fisher, who passed before this book was released. His last text message to me was, "LIVE YOUR DREAM." I read it often. I am still listening.

# CONTENTS

Acknowledgments .................................................................7
Foreword ..............................................................................9
Pockets ................................................................................11

Day 1:   Health Inspections ...............................................13
Day 2:   Options ................................................................15
Day 3:   Keep Talking .......................................................18
Day 4:   The Rain ..............................................................21
Day 5:   Breathe .................................................................24
Day 6:   Stuff Stinks ..........................................................27
Day 7:   Broken ..................................................................30
Day 8:   Chin Up, Shoulders Back ..................................33
Day 9:   Handstands ..........................................................36
Day 10: The Fly .................................................................39
Day 11: Danger ..................................................................41
Day 12: The Room ............................................................44
Day 13: The Chicken Sandwich ......................................47
Day 14: Exhausted .............................................................50
Day 15: The Bullies ...........................................................53

Day 16: Your Turn ...................................................56

Day 17: Plans for Spring ........................................59

Day 18: Your Next Move .......................................62

Day 19: Peanut Butter and Jelly ..........................65

Day 20: Preservation .............................................68

Day 21: The Juicer .................................................70

Day 22: Embarrassment ........................................73

Day 23: Darkness...................................................77

Day 24: Still Tripping ...........................................80

Day 25: The Big Kick ...........................................83

Day 26: Time..........................................................86

Day 27: Loneliness.................................................89

Day 28: Death ........................................................93

Day 29: The Raccoon ............................................96

Day 30: Abandoned Cart .....................................100

Day 31: God...........................................................103

Final Thought .......................................................107

# ACKNOWLEDGMENTS

Thank you to my extraordinary husband, BJ, for sending me on the staycation that allowed me to finish writing this book. Thank you to my brilliant sons, Elijah and Aaron, for teaming up with your dad to be my greatest supporters.

Thank you to Bishop Alfred A. Owens, for loving me as your own.

Thank you to Tricia, for your not-so-gentle nudges.

Thank you to everyone who has, and who continues to, pray for me.

I love you all.

# FOREWORD

We live in a day when despair exists in all parts of the world. Confusion, resentment, depression, and anguish are commonplace for millions of people. There is a great conquest to find a moment of relief, or to simply get a break, but so many of us just can't seem to find the beautiful light that we search for in a dark world. What we wish for is a day when pain, failure, and dejection no longer exist. What the world seeks for is hope.

Hope is the perspective that there is a glimmer of sunshine on the other side. Hope is the idea that things can turn around for better. Hope breeds confidence, strength, and encouragement. I have found some levels of hope in my family, friends, and colleagues. They have been there to support, comfort, and strengthen me. I find, however, that my greatest return on anything I have needed in life is my hope in Jesus Christ.

Hope is an act of faith. It is being crazy enough to believe that something better is there, although it is not apparent. The best hope that I have experienced is in the Word of God, which is the voice of God. I often tell people that when you are down and in despair, the only thing you need is a "God-said!" What is a God-said? I'm glad you asked! A God-said is anything God says from His word. The Bible tell us that God is not a man that He can lie, so if God said something, it will come to pass. You can cast your hope on God's word! Once you have a God-said, you can rest in knowing that this, too, shall pass, like things before it! You are going to be just fine when you discover hope.

I am so proud of my spiritual daughter, Ayesha. *A Pocket Full of Hope* is a wonderful read of every day anecdotes that express ways in which we can find hope in every situation. Let this book be your inspiration and remind you that when the world considers you a hopeless case, remember, through Christ, you are a case of hope.

—Bishop Alfred A. Owens, Jr.

# POCKETS

I love pockets, pockets on pants, pockets on shorts, pockets on skirts, and pockets on dresses. Who doesn't love a well-sized side pocket that gives your hands a place to rest when they are tired of being held up? They are the perfect place to keep your cellphone when you've got to turn the ringer off but keep it on vibrate so as not to miss that important call. I can't forget about that hidden pocket, the one that is well disguised within the fabric of one's clothing or backpack. The concept of the pocket is so brilliant. It is a way to protect items while maintaining easy access to them.

There is only one thing that irks me about pockets, and that is to see one pulled inside out. I am quite aware that this may read as a bit trivial, but the *purpose* of a pocket is to *hide* and to *hold*. A pocket that is pulled inside out does not serve its purpose; instead, it exposes its emptiness.

The simple image of pant pockets pulled inside out sends a message that the wearer is broke. In fact, the motions of pulling empty pockets out is a nonverbal way of communicating one's frustration with one's state of financial helplessness. It's another way of saying, "I have nothing."

My eldest son, in his haste to get dressed, will often put his pants on and ignore the obvious exposure of his empty pockets. I remember telling him one day to push his pockets in. His reply was, "But, Mommy, I don't even have anything in them." My response to him that day was, "You don't have anything in them right now, but one day, you will. I want you to practice wearing them the right way now so that, when that day comes, you'll be ready."

The message to my son on that day serves as the springboard and inspiration for this book. You may feel as though you have nothing right now, but be encouraged. One day that will change. Until then, I want you to hold on to hope. I want you to get into the habit of encouraging yourself. God does not operate according to our personal calendars and projections. Instead, He has given us the Bible to strengthen and uplift us, to keep our hearts and minds settled until He is ready to make His move. God gives us hope through His word. The Word of God is like a pocket. It protects our faith while allowing us access to it. It is our hiding place. It holds us together. We can place our hope in the Word of God. We can place hope in our pocket. In fact, when life tries to convince us that we are empty, we can be assured that we've got a pocket full of hope.

As you read, study, and meditate over the next thirty-one days, my prayer is that your faith in God increases daily. Even during those difficult times, when you want to give up, may you never let go of your determination to hold on to the promises of God. As you face your spiritual battles, may these pages serve as a tool that connects you to the Word of God. When the dust settles, may you emerge undefeated and still full of hope.

## DAY 1

# Health Inspections

Have you ever gone into a restaurant and right by its front entrance, posted on the wall, you see the public health inspection rating? Generally, it's a percentage, 100 being the best and 0 being the worst. I have never seen a top rating of 100, and I've been in some pretty fantastic restaurants. The highest rating that I've ever seen is 99 percent. Now while most would accept that as an excellent, almost perfect rating, my mind tends to wander and question that missing 1 percent. Why wasn't it perfect? Why didn't it get a 100 percent rating? Will that 1 percent be evident in the food that I am about to eat? Did the cook not wash his or her hands? Did they drop the food on the floor and replate it? Do they have critters living in the kitchen? Okay, that's a little extreme, but you get the idea. Almost perfect is not perfect!

### God does not fall short of perfection.

It would be pointless to encourage you to put all of your confidence in someone who has the potential to fail you. Even if that person had a 99 percent success rate, who is to say that your situation will not be that 1 percent failure? The good news is that God does not fall short of perfection. In fact, He can do everything but fail. Failure goes against the nature of God. He is not almost perfect; He is perfect. Rest assured that when you put your hope in God, He will work out everything that concerns you. The catch is that He doesn't always do things in the manner that we expect Him to. Actually, His ways are always better than ours. Go ahead and think about your most challenging situation and come up with a brilliant idea to solve it. As glorious as your solution may be, God can do better than that. You can trust Him.

## SUGGESTED READING

Ephesians 3:20–21 "Now to Him who is able to do far more abundantly beyond all that we ask or think, according to the power that works within us, to Him be the glory in the church and in Christ Jesus to all generations forever and ever. Amen."

Isaiah 55:10–11 "For as the rain and the snow come down from heaven, And do not return there without watering the earth And making it bear and sprout, And furnishing seed to the sower and bread to the eater; So will My word be which goes forth from My mouth; It will not return to Me empty, Without accomplishing what I desire, And without succeeding in the matter for which I sent it."

# DAY 2

# Options

Our family prays together every night before we go to sleep. Each of us is given a turn to pray from the heart. Our oldest had gotten himself into a little trouble one day. We had a talk with him about why he was in trouble and explained to him that he will often be presented with options. He will have to choose to do what he believes is right or what he believes is wrong. We never know how much of what we say is actually getting through to the children, but that night, in his prayers, he asked the Lord, "Please help my brother and me to make good choices."

## Hope is always an option.

Mark 5:25–34 tells the story of a woman who had been sick for twelve years. She had been to several physicians and exhausted all of her finances trying to get better. Instead of getting better, her condition got worse. She was out of options. Surely, she had reached a point of despair and settled for the conclusion that she would continue to be sick until the day she died.

Something happened one day though. The people around the town were talking about Jesus, the great healer and miracle worker. She heard that He had healed the blind and the lame; He had even raised the dead. Hearing about Jesus ignited her hope. Her hope told her that if she could somehow be in the right place, at the right time, when Jesus was passing by; all she would have to do is touch the hem of His clothing. Surely, with all of the supernatural power that He held, that touch alone would be enough to heal her of her condition.

When she noticed that the crowd was large and that there was no way she could simply walk to Jesus, she took the only remaining option, to push through the crowd and somehow grab a hold of Jesus's cloak. Immediately, the woman was healed.

When you get to that place where you don't have the luxury of multiple options, take a quick inventory of the things that your eyes don't easily see. You will find faith. You will find hope. You will find God. When your own solutions fail, when all earthly options prove unsuccessful, hope is always an option. The woman in this story had to wait until Jesus was passing. You don't have to wait; Jesus is always just a prayer away. As long as He is with us, we can have hope that when we call out to Him, He will answer us. You may not see Him physically, but if you reach out to Him, you will touch Him.

## SUGGESTED READING

Psalm 145:18 "The LORD is near to all who call upon Him, To all who call upon Him in truth."

Psalm 71:14 "But as for me, I will hope continually, And will praise You yet more and more."

# DAY 3

# Keep Talking

Weeks, days, and months leading up to the most anticipated boxing match of the year, we are inundated with commercials, press conferences, and interviews that give the fighters the opportunity to address each other and talk about the impending battle. It is during those times that we will hear the most trash talk possible. With intense confidence and courage, the competitors make declarations about their anticipated victory. With words like, "I will crush you" or "I will make you wish you never showed up," fighters let their opponents know that they mean business and that losing is not an option. The problem with this level of expectancy on both sides is that, ultimately, one competitor will be defeated, proving their words to be empty and fruitless. Not only does that put the loser in a humbling and embarrassing position, but in the moments that follow the fight, the loser is expected to make a follow-up statement to the press, detailing the failure.

## Don't let failure shut your mouth.

Peter was Jesus's most vocal disciple. When Jesus told the disciples that He would be crucified, Peter spoke up and said, "God forbid it, Lord! This shall never happen to You." (Matthew 16:22). When Jesus told Peter that he would deny Him before others, Peter said, "Even if I have to die with You, I will not deny You." (Matthew 26:35). When Jesus told the disciples, who were out fishing, to cast their nets on the other side, Peter said, "Master, we worked hard all night and caught nothing," (Luke 5:5), suggesting that there were no fish to be caught. After each of these instances, Peter's presumptions were proven to be wrong. Peter, like you and I, often failed. The wonderful thing about Peter was that failure did not cause him to shut his mouth. Peter had a future that was hinged on his determination to keep talking. After Jesus's resurrection and ascension, Peter used his mouth to preach his initial sermon, causing thousands of people to come to salvation through Jesus Christ.

You may have some promises that you've broken. Perhaps you've made some declarations that didn't pan out. You may have even had some trash talk sessions with the devil, and despite your proclamations, it seems like he has won the battle. Don't let failure shut your mouth. He may have won the battle, but in the end, if you stick with God, you will win the war. Just keep talking. Keep declaring the Word of God over your life. Keep speaking biblical truths over your future. Just like the boxer has to get back in the ring for the next fight, you too need to get back to living! Though it may not feel like it right now, your future is hinged on your determination to keep talking. When you start decreeing and declaring victory, know that you will be tested. The enemy will try to make you look like a liar and a fool but, stand firm. Don't give up. Don't shut up.

## SUGGESTED READING

Romans 8:37 "But in all these things we overwhelmingly conquer through Him who loved us."

Proverbs 18:21 "Death and life are in the power of the tongue, And those who love it will eat its fruit."

DAY 4

# The Rain

Rainfall occurs in a variation of strengths. While there are downpours that make it hard to see clearly while driving, sometimes the rain is so light, you can take your time to walk in it without worrying about your hair or clothes getting soaked. Sometimes the heat from the sun is so intense that, seconds after falling, the raindrops have already dried up on the ground. The challenge we face is that at the first prediction of rain, our minds begin to plan for all of the things that we suspect will go wrong. We make assumptions that obstacles are to follow. Traffic will be terrible. Plans may be cancelled. That is when we tend to make declarations that hold our thoughts captive, declarations like, "When it rains, it pours."

When it rains, it doesn't always pour.

The Bible tells us about the heaviest rainfall in history, one wherein it rained constantly for forty days and forty nights. God had become grieved with His creation, and with the sin and corruption that had infiltrated the earth. God determined that He would wipe the earth clean of all creatures but, "Noah found favor in the eyes of the LORD" (Genesis 6:8). God instructed Noah to build an ark so that when all of creation was extinguished, the lives of Noah, his family, and the selected pairs of every creature could take refuge in it. After the rain stopped falling, it took 150 days for the floods to dry up. The scriptures tell us that God remembered Noah and made a covenant with him, for all creatures and all future generations, that He would never again wipe out the earth with a flood. This covenant was in the form of the rainbow.

God's gift of the rainbow was a promise that, from that day forward, all of creation would survive. Every time you see a rainbow appear in the sky, it is a reminder that no matter what you have gone through, you have survived it. The extraordinary thing about the rainbow is that, in order for us to see it, there must be raindrops in the sky. Its beauty is expressed when light shines through the raindrops.

All that you are enduring right now may feel intolerable. It may seem like you have to face one ordeal after another. Perhaps, it is so constant that you are willing to accept any kind of escape as temporary relief from it all. It feels like more than any one person should have to deal with. Here's what I've learned: when it rains, it doesn't always pour. Be grateful for the heavy rain as well as the light showers. God is in the midst of them both. Both rainfalls have the potential to wipe the slate clean. Both can be the catalyst to a fresh start. Rest assured that, at some point, the warmth of the sun will serve as your indicator that the rain has subsided and the rainbow, as an indicator that there is still hope for your future.

## SUGGESTED READING

Lamentations 3:31–33 "For the Lord will not reject forever, For if He causes grief, Then He will have compassion According to His abundant lovingkindness. For He does not afflict willingly Or grieve the sons of men."

Joel 2:22–23 "Do not fear, beasts of the field, For the pastures of the wilderness have turned green, For the tree has borne its fruit, The fig tree and the vine have yielded in full. So rejoice, O sons of Zion, And be glad in the LORD your God; For He has given you the early rain for your vindication. And He has poured down for you the rain, The early and latter rain as before."

# DAY 5

# Breathe

This experience will be familiar to you as I am certain that I am not the only to have gone through it several times. I was quickly walking around the corner of the foot of the bed and in my haste, I misjudged the distance between its wooden legs and my foot. Without any warning of the excruciating pain that would follow, the bed attacked me. Some might say that, I stubbed my toe but, I prefer the dramatics of my recount. It sounds less clumsy. Never mind the details. My immediate reaction was a loud squeal, which was only suppressed by the sudden urge to hold my breath. I held it for about seven seconds before telling myself to just breathe. I exhaled. I refilled my lungs, inhaling, and then I slowly released that air again. The pain slowly subsided.

## Inhale, exhale.

Breathing is something that the body naturally does constantly throughout the day without any prompting from us, and without us having to give it instructions. We can sometimes control our breathing to slow down or speed up. We can even hold our breath, however, after doing so for a limited amount of time, our brains instinctively try to force our lungs to continue breathing. It is what our lungs were divinely designed to do. We have a tendency to hold our breath when we are afraid or nervous about something or when we are in pain, but ultimately, our lungs prevail. Our lungs fight against all outside interferences in order to do what they were created to do.

The psalmist gave the command in Psalm 150:6: "Let everything that has breath, praise the LORD." There are no conditions to this instruction. The scripture does not paint the picture of a bed of roses, nor of sunshine and butterflies. Instead, we are told that as long as we have the ability to breath, we ought to praise God.

We were created to glorify God. Just as our lungs fight against suppression in order to fulfill their purpose, we too must fight against our pain, our desperation, our anxieties, and our fears in order to fulfill our purpose. When we begin to breathe again, that is an indication that, regardless of what our bodies are enduring, our natural instincts are to keep living.

You may be dealing with some challenges right now that make you feel like you are suffocating. Perhaps you've been holding your breath, afraid of what will happen next. I challenge you to inhale, exhale, and repeat. You are still here. Do not give up. Do not stop breathing. You are not prone to quitting. On the contrary, you have been divinely designed to fight back. May every breath you take today fill your hope for a better tomorrow.

## SUGGESTED READING

1 Peter 5:10–11 "After you have suffered for a little while, the God of all grace, who called you to His eternal glory in Christ, will Himself perfect, confirm, strengthen and establish you. To Him be dominion forever and ever. Amen."

Matthew 6:26 "Look at the birds of the air, that they do not sow, nor reap nor gather into barns, and yet your heavenly Father feeds them. Are you not worth much more than they?"

Job 33:4 "The Spirit of God has made me, And the breath of the Almighty gives me life."

DAY 6

# Stuff Stinks

We live in the suburbs, but less than two miles away from several farms. We are so close to the farms, that we can often smell when the crops are being tended to with fresh fertilizer. It is a smell that would cause the unfamiliar nostrils to turn up in disdain. We have learned that the aroma, though often unpleasant, is an indication that extra care is being put into the produce and ultimately the livestock that are growing. In tending our own gardens, we learn that the best fertilizers are dirty and have the worst kind of stench; but when handled correctly, they can produce the biggest harvest. The smell is always the worst when they are fresh out of the bag. They are made out of animal and other compostable waste and they give off an instant odor, but they never produce instant results. Whatever has been planted, needs to be in that stinking dirt for a considerable amount of time before it starts to yield anything. The best fertilizers help to change to structure of the soil, making it more conducive to absorbing water and nutrients that help seeds grow. They produce, the good stuff.

# Good stuff comes out of stuff that stinks.

Naaman was the great commander of the army of Aram. He was valiant and well-respected, but he had leprosy. Elisha, the prophet of God, sent a word to Naaman, telling him to wash himself in the Jordan River, dipping in it seven times. This would cleanse Naaman's skin and heal him of leprosy. Naaman had a problem with these instructions because, of all of the many rivers around, the Jordan was the dirtiest one. Naaman couldn't understand why a man of his stature and prominence would need to go into such filthy waters. How could something so dirty have the ability to cleanse? How could something that stinks bring healing? It took some convincing, but eventually, Naaman did what the prophet told him to do by dipping himself in the Jordan river seven times. After the seventh dip, his flesh was clean and he was completely healed of the leprosy (2 Kings 5:1–14).

What you are going through may stink right now; there is no denying that. It's hard to comprehend why it has to be this way but, know that you've got to go through the process, so that God can produce something in you and through you. The reality of our condition has a way of humbling us, teaching us that we are not above the hardships that others face. Good stuff comes out of stuff that stinks. When you have come through, it will be so beautiful, so healthy, and so worth the wait. Regardless of what it looks like, feels like, or even smells like, hold on to the hope that the end result will be good.

## SUGGESTED READING

Psalm 27:13 "I would have despaired unless I had believed that I would see the goodness of the LORD in the land of the living. Wait for the LORD; Be strong and let your heart take courage; Yes, wait for the LORD."

Romans 8:28 "And we know that God causes all things to work together for good to those who love God, to those who are called according to His purpose."

# DAY 7

# Broken

Our sons do a wonderful job of purging their games and toys periodically. They make room on the floor and sort the items into three piles: the trash pile, the donation pile, and the keep pile. They have generous hearts and often give away the toys that we know still hold great value. They are so diligent in this process that we rarely need to examine their piles. We just trust that they know what they are doing, and we go along with it. After one of the more recent purge sessions, I noticed that the keep pile seemed higher than in times past. I decided to look through it to see if there was anything that could be pulled from it. I quickly realized that the items were not numerous, but they were large. I examined some of these large pieces and realized that, in different ways, they were all broken. I pointed out the broken pieces to the boys and asked them why they were keeping these toys. Their response was quick and simple, "We don't use them the same way anymore. We use those to build our skate park."

## Broken does not mean useless.

When the apostle Paul, along with the other prisoners and soldiers, were sailing to Rome, they encountered a storm. The storm caused a shipwreck. Because this happened at night, they had to wait until the morning to assess the situation. When daylight came, they realized that the ship had hit a sandbar and the bow was stuck. The impact caused pieces of the stern to break off. Some of the passengers were able to swim, so they jumped overboard and swam to shore. Those who were not able to swim, held on to the broken pieces of the ship and used them to get to land. Those broken pieces no longer served their purpose as part of the boat, but they were repurposed as lifesavers (Acts 27:27–44).

You may be living in a broken state right now. You may be suffering as a result of broken promises. Maybe things haven't gone the way that you planned, and what you thought was all together is now falling apart. God can use your brokenness to make something beautiful. Maybe He will build something new. Maybe He will use your experiences to bring you healing. Maybe your broken pieces will save someone's life. Don't discard your broken pieces. Broken does not mean useless.

## SUGGESTED READING

Isaiah 61:1b–3a "He has sent me to bind up the brokenhearted, To proclaim liberty to captives And freedom to prisoners; To proclaim the favorable year of the LORD And the day of vengeance of our God; To comfort all who mourn, To grant those who mourn in Zion, Giving them a garland instead of ashes, The oil of gladness instead of mourning, The mantle of praise instead of a spirit of fainting."

Psalm 147:3 "He heals the brokenhearted And binds up their wounds."

2 Corinthians 4:7–9 "But we have this treasure in earthen vessels, so that the surpassing greatness of the power will be of God and not from ourselves; we are afflicted in every way, but not crushed; perplexed, but not despairing; persecuted, but not forsaken; struck down, but not destroyed."

# DAY 8

# Chin Up, Shoulders Back

We try our best to instill good communication practices in our children. We teach them to look at people in the eyes when they are speaking, face the person that they are speaking with; keep their heads up. We remind them daily that they are destined for greatness and that they can accomplish anything that they put their minds and efforts toward accomplishing. We are determined to raise strong men who, no matter what limitations are presented to them, will see themselves as capable of breaking barriers of discrimination, inequality, and condemnation in order to fulfill their God-given purposes in life. Our goal is to raise children who are confident that, no matter what they face in life, the fact that they are facing it is the halfway point to victory.

## God sees you better than you see yourself.

A lack of confidence becomes dominant when a level of trust has been compromised, such as when you've put your trust in a friend and that friend betrays you, or when you trust that your vehicle will take you take to work, but it breaks down on the road. Failure and a lack of confidence go hand in hand. Moreover, it is difficult to have confidence in ourselves when we have disappointed ourselves over and over again. Whatever you are facing today, you are facing it. That means your head is up; keep it there. You're already winning.

When your head is up, your body follows suit with good posture. You know that you have good posture when the muscles in your body are strong with very little strain. This strength develops when you have spent a considerable amount of time sitting, standing, walking, and lying down properly. In fact, do any of those things incorrectly, and the negative consequences could take days, even weeks, to reverse.

Likewise, your hope increases when you spend time communicating with God through prayer and through reading His word. Regardless of what you have done or how far you have traveled from the path that you should be on, hope helps you to keep your chin up and shoulders back. Know that God sees you better than you see yourself. He hasn't changed his mind about you. His intentions toward you have always been, and still are, good.

## SUGGESTED READING

Jeremiah 29:11–13 "'For I know the plans that I have for you,' declares the LORD, 'plans for welfare and not for calamity to give you a future and a hope. Then you will call upon Me and come and pray to Me, and I will listen to you. You will seek Me and find Me when you search for Me with all your heart.'"

Psalm 73:26 "My flesh and my heart may fail, But God is the strength of my heart and my portion forever."

Romans 5:5 "and hope does not disappoint, because the love of God has been poured out within our hearts through the Holy Spirit who was given to us."

# DAY 9

# Handstands

I remember having to chair a strategic planning meeting many years ago. I was the first to arrive, and so I took my seat, opened a notebook, and waited. Truthfully, I have never enjoyed business meetings, and that one was no different. On top of that, I woke up that morning in a "nothing will satisfy me today" mood; I had no intention of perking up at all. I was dealing with the destruction of what I thought would have been lifelong relationships. I was hurt, angry, and just plain disappointed with the hand that I was dealt in various areas of my life. I had already fixed my mind and my body language to communicate my lack of interest in being present, period. As the participants filed in one by one, I greeted each with a low-key, inauthentic greeting. The meeting commenced, and after a few moments with my obvious lack of participation, one of my coworkers asked me the dreaded question, "Are you okay? Is something bothering you?" My response, of course, was in the affirmative because I didn't want to invite anyone to my pity party. I just wanted to be left alone in it. I will never forget the words that followed. He said to me, "Your mood is off today, and when your mood is off it throws the room off. You are a giver. That's just one of your strengths. You give off vibes that set the tone for those around you. When you are off, it makes it hard for the rest of us." I have never told him this, but those words changed my life.

# Hope is contagious.

Let's face it; some days are just a write-off. Rather than trying to fix everything that went wrong, we would do better to pretend the day never happened and look forward to another attempt tomorrow. Those are the days that I don't want to say hello. I don't want to say good night. I certainly don't want to make anyone else smile, not initially anyway. Here's what I've learned though: regardless of how horrible I feel, when I do say hello, when I do say good night, and when I can make someone else smile, I feel so much better. Those words and actions are, in my own way, sharing the message of hope with the receiver. I'm letting that person know that I notice them. I am letting someone know that he or she is not alone, and even if I am the only other person around, my presence has at least doubled their chances of survival.

You can give hope. The challenge comes when you don't feel like you have anything to give. It is in those times that you need to dig deep and command your mood to line up with the message of hope. Every day, our words and actions send a message to those around us. What if I told you that, in spite of how you may feel today, you have the power to encourage someone else? Do you know that hope is contagious? Do you know that you can set the tone for your environment? It is not always easy. Sometimes, you've got to do a handstand in order to turn your frown into a smile. That handstand will probably make you feel better too. It will show you how strong and capable you actually are.

## SUGGESTED READING

Romans 5:1–5 "Therefore, having been justified by faith, we have peace with God through our Lord Jesus Christ, through whom also we have obtained our introduction by faith into this grace in which we stand; and we exult in hope of the glory of God. And not only this, but we also exult in our tribulations, knowing that tribulation brings about perseverance; and perseverance, proven character; and proven character, hope; and hope does not disappoint, because the love of God has been poured out within our hearts through the Holy Spirit who was given to us."

1 Samuel 30:6 "Moreover David was greatly distressed because the people spoke of stoning him, for all the people were embittered, each one because of his sons and his daughters. But David strengthened himself in the LORD his God."

DAY 10

# The Fly

Fear is something that doesn't have to be taught in order for us to react to it. We often laugh about our youngest son and his quick reflexes when faced with the slightest indication of danger. If he were a character in a horror movie, he would be the one that survives to tell the story because he wouldn't stick around long enough to be killed. At the first sign of blood, sound of a scream, or rumble in the ground, he would not look to the left nor to the right; he would simply run. He would not stop running until he has found safety. For years, he had a terrible fear of anything smaller than him; anything that crawled, slithered, or flew, he wanted nothing to do with it. One particularly terrifying encounter was with a fly. The fly buzzed around his head and just the sound of it alone made him scream. The swiftness of the fly made it hard to see, but eventually, it stopped zipping around and landed on the table in front of him. Just as he was getting ready to run away, I held him close and asked him what I thought would be a life-changing question: "Who is bigger, you or the fly?" I explained to him that although the fly was fast and its buzzing was loud, the fly could not harm him. He was bigger, stronger, and smarter than the fly. The most that the fly could do was try to intimidate him. I think I lost the three-year-old's attention at that point. He squirmed out of my arms and ran away.

## You are bigger than the intimidation.

The Bible tells us in 2 Timothy 1:7 that God has not given us the spirit of fear, yet so many of us deal with fear on a daily basis. Where does fear come from? Fear comes from situations or people that move about in an intimidating manner. We can conquer our fear with hope. Hope tells us that, although what we are facing is intimidating, we are bigger than it. Hope tells us that we have power, love, and a sound mind, given to us by God. With these things, we are unstoppable.

Don't let your fears dictate how you see yourself or your future. You are bigger than your situation. You are bigger than your past. You are bigger than the intimidation. You are bigger than the negative words that buzz around your ears like a pesky fly.

## SUGGESTED READING

1 John 4:4 "You are from God, little children, and have overcome them; because greater is He who is in you than he who is in the world."

Philippians 4:13 "I can do all things through Him who strengthens me."

## DAY 11

# Danger

I've always wanted to go skydiving. If I could guarantee that nothing could possibly go wrong, I would absolutely, probably, maybe go with no hesitation. My fear of this adventure lies solely in the level of danger and the possibility of injury and/or death. Take away the fear of danger, and there would be nothing hindering me. Then again, if danger is no longer an element, I wonder if the activity would be exciting and enjoyable. I know for certain that the only way I would go through with it is if I believe that, although it is scary, there are enough safety precautions in place to ensure that I come out of the experience alive. I've got to believe that even if I get some bumps and bruises, I will be able to look back on the experience and know that I conquered my fears. I will be able to reflect on it, having realized a dream come true.

Hope is risky.

The three Hebrew boys—Shadrach, Meshach, and Abednego—knew that the stance they were taking against the king's orders was a dangerous one. They knew that it came attached to a death sentence. They also knew that there was a difference between a sentence from man, and a sentence from God. These young men made up in their minds that, if they were thrown into a fiery furnace because of their godly principles, the God that they served would deliver them. Their convictions were so strong that they concluded, even if God did not rescue them, they would still stand by their beliefs, and they would not bow down to anyone or anything other than God (Daniel 3). The fear of danger would have led them to give into the king's demands, but hope led them to trust God in the presence of danger. They were taking a huge risk by standing on their beliefs. The risk paid off; the angel of the Lord was present with the boys in the fiery furnace, and they survived, completely unscathed and without any burns.

Hope is risky, but it is most fulfilling when we place it in the Lord. Much like skydiving, we've got to believe that the Lord has provided safety features to keep us while we go forward in life. Like the three Hebrew boys, we've got to trust that, even if He doesn't rescue us in the way that we foresee it, it is better to be obedient to Him and His call than to give into the fears that life presents. If we run from the risk, we will never see the reward.

## SUGGESTED READING

Daniel 3:16–18 "Shadrach, Meshach and Abed-nego replied to the king, 'O Nebuchadnezzar, we do not need to give you an answer concerning this matter. If it be so, our

God whom we serve is able to deliver us from the furnace of blazing fire; and He will deliver us out of your hand, O king. But even if He does not, let it be known to you, O king, that we are not going to serve your gods or worship the golden image that you have set up.'"

Psalm 25:3 "Indeed, none of those who wait for You will be ashamed; Those who deal treacherously without cause will be ashamed."

Psalm 20:7 "Some boast in chariots and some in horses, But we will boast in the name of the LORD, our God."

## DAY 12

# The Room

Have you ever walked into a room, and within five minutes of being there, an overwhelming feeling of inadequacy drenched you? It didn't take long for you to realize that your degrees didn't add up, your career didn't line up, and your bank account didn't match up with those around you. I have been in innumerable situations wherein I have felt totally inadequate. Sometimes, it was while sitting at a banquet table with people who rank higher than me, knowing that I lack the experiences to share in the conversation. Other times, I was among groups of women who were very familiar with each other and showed no interest in expanding their clique to include me. Have you ever attended a function that you knew you were on the B-list for? Meaning, you only got invited because some A-listers declined and so more space opened up. I have. During those times, I would ask myself the question, "Why am I here? Do I even deserve to be in this room?"

## Don't let your fear of inadequacy stop you from showing up.

1 Samuel 16 tells the story of the prophet Samuel going to Jesse's home to anoint the future king of Israel. The scripture tells us that Jesse brought seven sons into the room before Samuel, and one by one, Samuel turned them away, indicating that none of them were chosen by God to be king. There was, however, one more son that Jesse did not invite into the room, David, the youngest son and shepherd boy that worked in the field. David was probably used to being excluded from the things that his older brothers participated in. He was probably seen as the weakest boy and the one that was the least qualified for the position. He wasn't invited in because no one believed that he was good enough.

Samuel sent for David to come inside. I can only imagine how David must have felt when he was the last one to arrive to that party that he wasn't on the A-list for. I believe that there was doubt on all sides that he was the chosen one, yet when he stood before Samuel, the Lord said, "Arise, anoint him; for this is he" (1 Samuel 16:12).

When God calls you to the room, don't let your fear of inadequacy stop you from showing up. Regardless of your level of education, your social status, your finances, or your appearance, you are a valuable asset to God's plan for this world. You may look at those around you and feel small, but hope says that you are special in God's eyes, and He will reveal His purpose for your life. You have experiences and testimonies that are unique to you. You have something that you can contribute to the earth. There is no doubt about it; you deserve to be in the room.

## SUGGESTED READING

1 Samuel 16:7b "for God sees not as man sees, for man looks at the outward appearance, but the LORD looks at the heart."

Romans 8:30–31 "and these whom He predestined, He also called; and these whom He called, He also justified; and these whom He justified, He also glorified. What then shall we say to these things? If God is for us, who is against us?"

## DAY 13

# The Chicken Sandwich

I have a favorite place that I like to go to for what is probably the best chicken sandwich ever made. When I was first introduced to this place, I went there almost every day for lunch. I am not exaggerating. Every day. It was just that good. My family went on a weekend road trip out of town, and during one of our stops, we visited another location of this amazing place. I just knew it was going to be good; it always was. Unfortunately, after one huge bite into the sandwich, I was devastated at the realization that the chicken was bad. I had never tasted anything so sour and old before. I returned the sandwich to the counter and let them know what the problem was. They offered to replace it, but it was too late. The experience was so traumatic for me. I didn't want to try another sandwich. If the one that I had was bad, chances are, all of the others in their stock would have been bad too. That decision made sense at that time.

Fast forward to our return home from the road trip. I went back to work. I should have gone back to my regular lunch routine at my favorite chicken spot, but I just couldn't do it. Although this was not the location of the bad chicken, my mind would not allow me to get past the fear of eating spoiled food again. I decided then that I was never going to buy that chicken sandwich, from any location, ever again. My husband tried to help me understand how unreasonable I was being. I even tried to talk myself out of the decision several times but couldn't. One day, by what must have been divine intervention, I received a coupon for a free meal at this used-to-be-my-favorite spot. I tried to ignore it. I wanted to give it away, but it just sat there on my desk, staring at me for days. Eventually, I told myself that I might as well go ahead and use it. If the chicken was bad, at least I wouldn't have wasted money on it. It was free! As for the bad taste, well, that was nothing that a fresh cup of sweet tea couldn't wash away. So I did it. One whole year after the initial incident, I tried again. Much to my delight, it was as though I was never wronged. That was the best chicken sandwich I had ever had, even better than the first!

## Your next try could be the one with the best results.

You may find yourself in a situation where that one thing or one person that you could always count on has failed you. The disappointment is, no doubt, devastating. It feels horrible and has left a bad taste in your mouth. So much so, that you don't ever want to try again. You need to know today that, just because things went awry before, doesn't mean that is how it will always be. Every person is different. Every situation is different. Don't give up hope that your next experience can be wonderful, just because of that one time, or several times, when you were let down. Your next effort could be the one where God intervenes and presents you with just what you need. Your next try could be the one with the best results. What do you have to lose? Hoping for better next time won't cost you anything. It's like a great coupon. Hope is free!

## SUGGESTED READING

I want to leave you with Psalm 34:8 "O taste and see that the LORD is good; How blessed is the man who takes refuge in Him!" because I think that's a funny way to end this story, but I will add to that Isaiah 43:18–19 "Do not call to mind the former things, Or ponder things of the past. Behold, I will do something new, Now it will spring forth; Will you not be aware of it? I will even make a road-way in the wilderness, Rivers in the desert."

## DAY 14

# Exhausted

My husband started exercising. Within weeks of doing so, he was dropping pounds, inches and gaining muscle. In efforts to catch up with him, I decided to join him at the gym. I had no idea where to start this fitness journey, so I decided that I would just follow his lead and claim the treadmill beside him. After a little guidance from him, I began walking. The brisk walk progressed to a light jog, and eventually, I set a good pace for myself. It was in the next few moments that I discovered, in addition to my food and pet dander allergies, I had yet another allergy. I most certainly was allergic to exercise. My skin became extremely itchy, and no matter how much I scratched, there was no relief. I quickly got off of the treadmill in a panic, and in an attempt to sooth my now fiery skin, I began drinking, no, gulping water. Seeing my distress, my husband got off of his treadmill and rushed over to me. I explained my symptoms to him—my burning, itchy skin—which, at that point, I was pressing the cold water bottle against. I felt extremely weak in my body; a feeling that could only be explained with my summarizing, "I'm exhausted." My husband's next words to me were encouraging and gave me a sense of self-awareness. "Dear," he said, "you're not allergic to exercise. That's just sweat. Your body is just not used to this workout, but it will adjust and get stronger. This will get better."

# You are capable of continuing on.

When the Israelites went to battle against the Amalekites in Exodus 17, though it was physical for the Israelites, it was also spiritual and reliant on the power of God that moved whenever Moses held up his staff. "Whenever Moses held up his hand, Israel prevailed, and whenever he lowered his hand, Amalek prevailed" (Exodus 17:11). The problem was that Moses's hands got tired. It became difficult for him to keep them lifted on his own. The scriptures tell us that after giving him a stone to sit on, Aaron and Hur stood beside Moses and held up his hands for him until sundown. This clinched the victory for the Israelites.

We can have the best of intentions to continue on our journey without looking back, without quitting, but the reality remains that we, in our humanity, get tired. We get tired of the pressure to provide. We grow weary of the expectations that others have placed on our success. The weight of our self-imposed deadlines for our life is enough to keep us from getting out of bed in the mornings. Hope lets us know that, when we are exhausted, God will give us strength. Sometimes, He sends it though the helping hands of others. Sometimes, He sends it supernaturally and miraculously. Rest assured that what you are feeling is not abnormal; you are capable of continuing on. Your body will get stronger. Things will get better.

## SUGGESTED READING

Isaiah 40:31 "Yet those who wait for the LORD Will gain new strength; They will mount up with wings like eagles, They will run and not get tired, They will walk and not become weary."

Galatians 6:9 "Let us not lose heart in doing good, for in due time we will reap if we do not grow weary."

DAY 15

# The Bullies

Halfway through the second grade of elementary school, our oldest son decided that he wanted to switch schools; he wanted to attend a French immersion school. As we were then, we are still amazed at the level of confidence and bravery that he has. After much consideration, he got his wish and started at his new school, at the beginning of the second term. The first few weeks were challenging, not because of the workload, but because he had become the new kid and was being bullied by other students. We realized very quickly that we needed to equip both he and his brother with the tools to stand up to bullies and perhaps even influence them for the better. It is usually the smartest child or the least intelligent child, the most unique-looking, the one that is new to the school, the one who receives special treatment from the teacher or the one that is always ignored; those are the ones that are often singled out and picked on. Very rarely do average children who fit the world's definition of normal, get picked on. As adults, it's those who quickly rise to leadership positions, those who appear to have more prominence, and those who are quite simply different, that are often targeted and yes, even in adulthood, they are bullied. Bullies thrive on making their victims feel as though they are less valuable than they really are. Bullies succeed when they have convinced their victims that simply being themselves is not enough, and that it will only lead to failure.

# You are not normal and that's a good thing.

Though Daniel is most famous as a result of his spending a night in a den of lions and coming out unscathed; his full story is actually one of surviving being bullied. Daniel, grew up during a time when his people were living in exile from Jerusalem. The king of Babylon decided that he wanted to recruit some of the young men of Israel who were intelligent, good looking, and skillful to work in his palace. Among those elite recruits, were Daniel and his buddies. The scriptures tell us that Daniel was faithful and that he had an excellent spirit. Daniel very quickly impressed the king by his gift of interpreting dreams and was elevated to powerful positions in the kingdom. The problem was that those who had served the king for years, prior to Daniel's arrival, became jealous of the success of this newcomer and they determined to bully him into self-destruction. The threat of being thrown into the lion's den was an attempt to intimidate and bully Daniel into going against his beliefs. Daniel, however, stood his ground and emerged victorious (Daniel 1–6).

You may be a victim of bullying right now. Perhaps you have always been quiet, reserved, and unassuming but yet you have received such favor in your life that you always get attention. God has chosen you before laying the foundations of the earth and even in your youth, you have been set apart for His purposes. You are not normal and that's a good thing. It is possible that as an adult, you can try your best to follow the Lord's instructions and live according to His word, yet find yourself constantly warding off the attacks of people around you. Do not be afraid. Do not turn away from God. Do not allow intimidation to keep you from being you. Hope says that you will survive the threats of your conspirators, and that they will look at your life as an example of how God protects His children.

## SUGGESTED READING

Daniel 6:22 "My God sent His angel and shut the lions' mouths and they have not harmed me, inasmuch as I was found innocent before Him; and also toward you, O king, I have committed no crime."

Psalm 91:11 "For He will give His angels charge concerning you, To guard you in all your ways."

## DAY 16

# Your Turn

If you have lived any time on this earth, then you have had your "When will it be my turn?" moment. I remember being in my late teens, sitting down with my girlfriends, laying out the timeline for our lives. My plan was to be married by the age of twenty-two, have all of my children by the age of twenty-eight, and be planning for retirement from my work by the age of fifty. I distinctly remember the consensus among my friends that I would probably be first to marry before all of them. Well, as we got older, lo and behold, one by one, my girlfriends started getting married and having babies while I was nowhere near that path. Instead of me posing the question, I found myself on the receiving end of, "When will it be your turn?"

Your time will not always match God's time.

A POCKET FULL OF HOPE

1 Samuel, chapter 1 tells the story of Hannah and Peninnah, the two wives of a man named Elkanah. Peninnah had many children for Elkanah, but Hannah had none. Peninnah would constantly taunt and provoke Hannah over her inability to have children. This went on for years, as Peninnah had more and more children. The torment was so intense that Hannah ultimately sank into a state of depression; she spent her days crying and would not eat. Although Hannah had not birthed any children for Elkanah, the scriptures tell us that he would give her a double portion of whatever he gave Peninnah simply because he loved her so much. This was not enough to soothe Hannah's desire for her turn to come. At her lowest point, Hannah went to the temple and poured out her heart before the Lord. She made a vow that, if God would give her a son, she would dedicate his life back to the Lord. The Lord spoke through the priest Eli and told Hannah that her petition would be granted. We later read that "in due time Hannah conceived and bore a son, and she called his name Samuel, for she said, 'I have asked for him from the Lord'" (1 Samuel 1:20 ESV).

The waiting season is a difficult one. We question ourselves, "Is something wrong with me?" "Am I being punished?" "Am I not deserving?" If we allow our minds to go there, we have the potential to create all kinds of wild justifications for life not going the way we want or expect it to go. On top of our own expectations, we add the expectations of family and friends: "When are you getting married?" After they are satisfied with our marital state, "When are you going to have children?" After the first child, "When will you have another child?" The pressure

57

can seem unending, and the well-intentioned concern only adds to our anxiety.

Thankfully, I didn't allow the pressures to coerce me into making hasty decisions and going down the wrong path, although there were several tempting opportunities. My testimony is that I waited on God. Let my testimony encourage you. One amazing husband and two beautiful sons later, I can look back and say that had I rushed to do things in my original timeline, I would not be who or where I am today. Just as God opened Hannah's womb in due time, I had a due time, and you do too. Your time will not always match God's time, but if you wait on Him, you will get your turn.

## SUGGESTED READING

Lamentations 3:24 "'The LORD is my portion,' says my soul, 'Therefore I have hope in Him.'"

Proverbs 16:9 "The mind of man plans his way, But the LORD directs his steps."

Proverbs 19:21 "Many plans are in a man's heart, But the counsel of the LORD will stand."

## DAY 17

# Plans for Spring

I had been looking at the calendar for weeks, just to remind myself of its arrival. The meteorologist let us know that since the groundhog saw his shadow, we had six more weeks of winter. Nevertheless, according to our calendars, March 21 would officially be day 1 of the spring season. Finally, we would be able to pack away our winter hats, scarves, and snowsuits. As a family, we look forward to the season change that gives the children the opportunity to ride their bikes outside and go to the skateboard park. At long last, we would be able to open the windows, let in the crisp air, and get our spring cleaning done. Springtime is our fresh start. It's the time for us to plant new flowers and plants. We start to see the tree buds bloom. The birds return from their winter retreat. It is the culmination of the cold days and long nights and the beginning of warmer and longer days.

Hope is a reminder that change will come.

When the first day of spring arrived, our great anticipation was matched with below freezing temperatures, strong winds, and the prediction of possible snow flurries. Spring looked nothing like what we were expecting. I bundled up and walked the children to school, and as I was walking back home, another parent turned to me and said, "So much for the first day of spring! What happened? Why is it so cold out here?"

In 1 Kings 18, in the midst of drought and famine, God told Elijah that the rain was about to fall. Elijah then told Ahab to get ready because he heard the sound of rain coming. The problem was that when Elijah sent his servant to go up to the mountaintop and look to the skies, he reported back that there was no indication of any rain on the way. He asked his servant to go back and look seven times. The Lord said the rain was on the way, but there were no signs of it at all. It was only on the seventh trip up the mountain that the servant was able to see a small cloud the size of a man's hand. This small cloud, along with the promise from God, was all that Elijah needed to assure him that rain was indeed about to fall. Shortly afterward, the heavy rain showers began.

The reality of seasons changing is that we mark those changes according to scientific calculations and manmade calendars. God, however, is not bound to our timelines. 2 Peter 3:8 (ESV) says, "with the Lord one day is as a thousand years, and a thousand years as one day." That means that we cannot expect God to operate under the parameters of time that we have set. Instead, He gives us His word, and we place our hopes in the belief that His word will accomplish all that it has set out to accomplish, in His time.

The calendar indicates when the season has changed, but when we look at the weather, it sometimes demonstrates the opposite. Similarly, seasons change in our lives but our circumstances seem to indicate otherwise. Although you may not see evidence of your change, nor feel the effects of the change right away, hope is a reminder that change will come. Perhaps you've made plans based on what you expected should have happened for you by now. You may be disappointed because your situation remains the same and you can't see any signs of improvement. Be encouraged. If it's your new season, things are about to change.

## SUGGESTED READING

Isaiah 55:11–12 "So will My word be which goes forth from My mouth; It will not return to Me empty, without accomplishing what I desire, And without succeeding in the matter for which I sent it. For you will go out with joy And be led forth with peace; The mountains and the hills will break forth into shouts of joy before you, And all the trees of the field will clap their hands."

Proverbs 16:9 "The mind of man plans his way, But the LORD directs his steps."

## DAY 18

# Your Next Move

Hope is both a thing that you can hold on to and an action that you can make. You can have hope in your heart while hoping with your heart. You will not stumble across hope. Hope is intentional. Hope speaks in the midst of silence and in the midst of noise. You must act because of it, move forward with it, and consciously pursue it.

Reading through these pages, you will discover that there are many reasons to hold on to hope. Your mind, however, will continuously be presented with reasons to do just the opposite. There will always be a fear that feels unconquerable and pain that feels intolerable. Each day will challenge you by presenting an easy way out, one that goes against the assurance that you have resting inside of you. You will be prompted to decide; either you allow fear to paralyze you, or you jump into the vehicle of hope, powered by desperation and with a destination set at peace.

## God has brought you this far; the next move is up to you.

In Joshua 24, the Lord spoke through Joshua, to the children of Israel. He reminded them about their history and how He continuously delivered them throughout the years. The Lord freed them from the bondage of Egypt, and when the Egyptians pursued them, the Lord drowned them in the Red Sea. The Lord caused them to be victorious over the Amorites. When Balak wanted to curse Israel, the Lord caused Balaam to bless them instead. God reminded Israel that He is the one who enabled them to defeat their enemies. He said, "I gave you a land on which you had not labored, and cities which you had not built, and you have lived in them; you are eating of vineyards and olive groves which you did not plant" (Joshua 24:13).

After reminding them of the power, love, and mercy of their God, Joshua then presented them with the opportunity to make a choice. They could either trust in the Lord, who had brought them this far, or they could serve a false god. This decision would have required them to turn away from everything that went against the knowledge of God. There was no room for compromise. They had to fully commit to obeying God and living for Him. Joshua made up in his mind, "as for me and my house, we will serve the Lord" (Joshua 24:15).

After everything that you have endured in your life, you are still here, alive, and reading these pages. You are still here because of the Lord, who, even when you didn't realize it, was holding you in His arms and carrying you. God has brought you this far; the next move is up to you. You can either trust in Him and place your hope for a better future in Him, or you can leave your life up to chance. God desires that you choose Him. He wants to continue to show you His love and power.

## SUGGESTED READING

Psalm 71:14 "But as for me, I will hope continually, And will praise You yet more and more."

Psalm 33:20–22 "Our soul waits for the LORD; He is our help and our shield. For our heart rejoices in Him, Because we trust in His holy name. Let Your lovingkindness, O LORD, be upon us, According as we have hoped in You."

Lamentations 3:21–23 "This I recall to my mind, Therefore I have hope. The LORD's loving kindnesses indeed never cease, For His compassions never fail. They are new every morning; Great is Your faithfulness. The LORD is my portion, 'says my soul, Therefore I have hope in Him.'"

## DAY 19

# Peanut Butter and Jelly

I remember so clearly the day that our oldest discovered his love for the peanut butter and jelly sandwich. Alright, love may be a strong word. Truth is, he finally agreed to try it and, after doing so, decided that he liked it but not as much as he liked grilled cheese sandwiches. My husband and I make great efforts to convince the children to love our childhood favorites. Unfortunately, those efforts are often fruitless and often culminate with us questioning, "Who doesn't love a peanut butter and jelly sandwich?" Of course, with the rise of nut allergies, it wouldn't be a wise menu item for everyone.

Nevertheless, for reasons of comparison, faith and hope go together like peanut butter and jelly. When you sandwich them together, they merge into one delicious explosion of flavor and become difficult to separate from each other. Rather than trying to define faith on its own, it would benefit us to see faith as a form of hope. If hope were water, faith would be an ice cube. When hope is intentionally poured out and placed in the conditions to solidify it, the result is faith. Just as ice cannot exist without water, "faith, if it has no works, is dead" (James 2:17). Hope says there is a possibility that this water may freeze. Faith says that there is an expectation of ice even before it has finished the process.

## In the end, we will win.

Sometimes our condition doesn't present us with options that we can see clearly. We hope that things will work out in our best interests, but we don't know what that looks like. That's when our faith in the Lord kicks in. We don't always know the specific plan that God has for us, but we do know that His plan will be in line with His word. Our faith, therefore, ought to be based on the Word of God. When we attach the scriptures to our various situations, we can stand firm that no matter what the process is, in the end we will win.

Whatever challenges you are facing today, know that change is possible. Allow your hope to materialize into faith. See yourself the way God sees you, as a survivor, as a winner. Here are some scriptures that you can read out loud to affirm yourself and confirm your victory:

Romans 8:28 "And we know that God causes all things to work together for good to those who love God, to those who are called according to His purpose."

2 Corinthians 4:7–10 "But we have this treasure in earthen vessels, so that the surpassing greatness of the power will be of God and not from ourselves; we are

afflicted in every way, but not crushed; perplexed, but not despairing; persecuted, but not forsaken; struck down, but not destroyed; always carrying about in the body the dying of Jesus, so that the life of Jesus also may be manifested in our body."

## SUGGESTED READING

Romans 8:37 "But in all these things we overwhelmingly conquer through Him who loved us."

1 John 5:4 "For whatever is born of God overcomes the world; and this is the victory that has overcome the world—our faith."

Revelation 21:3–4 "And I heard a loud voice from the throne, saying, 'Behold, the tabernacle of God is among men, and He will dwell among them, and they shall be His people, and God Himself will be among them, and He will wipe away every tear from their eyes; and there will no longer be any death; there will no longer be any mourning, or crying, or pain; the first things have passed away.'"

# DAY 20

# Preservation

The dilemma we face as people with hope, is that there is a chance that what we are hoping for may not ever manifest. We hope that God will heal us, yet we continue to suffer with our illnesses. We hope that we will find love and get married, but we spend what seems like a lifetime single. We hope that we will fit in with the norm in order that we not feel the sting of loneliness, but no matter how we try, we never feel accepted. What if there is no resolve? What if what we are believing in is something that we will never see?

> He will preserve you while you're in it.

The apostle Paul had a similar challenge. He had devoted his life to serving God and teaching the Gospel of Jesus Christ. Paul taught that we ought to have "fixed our hope on the living God, who is the Savior of all men, especially of believers" (1 Timothy 4:10), yet Paul, too, faced the disappointment of an unrealized expectation. He refers to his challenge as a thorn in his flesh. Paul petitioned to God with the hope that the thorn would leave him. Instead of a rescue mission, God met Paul's hope with a promise of preservation. God said, "My grace is sufficient for you, for power is perfected in weakness" (2 Corinthians 12:9). Paul then resolved to continue living out his assignment and destiny, knowing that God would be present with him and strengthen him throughout every difficult situation.

You may be waiting and hoping for something right now that has been taking so long; you don't know if it will ever happen. Truthfully, I cannot promise you that everything will work out the way that you expect it to, but I can promise you that the Bible is true. Just as God granted Paul the grace to survive, He has that same gift for you. God may not pull you out of your situation, but He will preserve you while you're in it. The other wonderful promise that we can rest on is that even when our expectations fail, God's will always prevails, and most assuredly, His plans are always better than ours.

## SUGGESTED READING

Psalm 119:49–50 (NIV) "Remember your word to your servant, for you have given me hope. My comfort in my suffering is this: Your promise preserves my life."

Isaiah 55:8–12 "'For My thoughts are not your thoughts, Nor are your ways My ways,' declares the LORD. "'For as the heavens are higher than the earth, So are My ways higher than your ways And My thoughts than your thoughts.'"

## DAY 21

# The Juicer

My husband has a bit of an addiction to buying gadgets and small appliances. If it's electronic and helps you stay connected, he's going to get it. If it makes cooking or baking easier or allows for more creativity in the kitchen, he wants it. Since I am not as technologically savvy and I'm not the one that does the majority of the cooking, I generally don't get in the way of his purchases. In fact, most of my birthday and special occasion gifts to him will contribute to the collections. I will never forget the year when he purchased the juicer. It was a fancy one, stainless steel, very sturdy. Juicing was the newest fad. Everyone was juicing everything. Fruits, veggies, potato skins, the works. At first, he was the only one using it in the home, but after some time, I got in on the action. I started with carrots, experimenting to come up with the perfect carrot juice. It started out strong, as most fads do, a couple of times per week. Gradually, I cut back and made carrot juice only once per week, especially since I was the only person drinking it. The last time that I used the juicer, I made the mistake of not cleaning it out right away. I pushed it to the back of the counter with the intention of getting back to it later that evening. Days went by and I totally forgot that it even needed to be cleaned. In fact, I didn't remember it until the following week when I pulled it to the front of the counter to use it again. By that time, the residue of the carrots had transformed into an absolutely disgusting, moldy, gray and green fungus. If the appearance wasn't enough to make my stomach do flips, when I opened the lid, the foulest odor immediately filled the air. If you haven't already figured me out by now, after reading these pages, then I'll just let you know; I had no choice but to toss the whole juicer away.

## You can be bigger and better than you've ever been.

Joshua 2 tells the story of a woman named Rahab. She is introduced to us as a prostitute. When we get further into the story, we learn that she had a father, mother, and siblings whom she loved and cared for, but all of that was overshadowed by the label of "harlot" that she had been given. Joshua sent two spies out to assess the Promised Land prior to them infiltrating it. The spies found refuge in Rahab's home. She hid them, protected them, and redirected their enemies away from them. In exchange for her help, she received a promise that she and her family would be safe from all harm when the Israelites took over the land. The beauty of Rahab's story is in the discovery that the label she was given did not confine her to mediocrity. Instead, she became a hero and a deliverer. Rahab went on in life to marry an Israelite and give birth to Boaz. Rahab's lineage made her an ancestor of King David and, ultimately, Jesus Christ.

I used the juicer often, until I started to get tired of it. Then when I decided that it was disgusting, I threw it away. I didn't want to spend the time nor the effort to clean it up. With us, God does just the opposite. I am so glad that God does not discard us as worthless when we appear tarnished and unusable. In fact, God is pleased to take us from our filthy state, cleanse us, and use our lives for His purpose. You do not have to live according to the labels that anyone has placed on you or that you have placed on yourself. You can be bigger and better than you've ever been. Your past doesn't imprison your future, unless you let it. You can choose to break free from that control. Hope says that your best days are still ahead of you and that your life will matter for generations to come.

## SUGGESTED READING

Isaiah 1:18 "'Come now, and let us reason together,' Says the LORD, 'Though your sins are as scarlet, They will be as white as snow; Though they are red like crimson, They will be like wool.'"

2 Corinthians 5:17 "Therefore if anyone is in Christ, he is a new creature; the old things passed away; behold, new things have come."

# DAY 22

# Embarrassment

I have had so many embarrassing moments that I had a hard time deciding which one to share with you. I thought about the time when I was on vacation with some girlfriends. We were on a guided tour that ended up in a body of water at the foot of a waterfall. I was looking extra cute in my two-piece bathing suit. Unfortunately, the bathing suit was through with me for the day because, when I decided to take one more dip underwater, I emerged, but the top of the bathing suit didn't. Every tour guide and fellow vacationer got a flash. As horrific as that experience was, I got over it, and I can even laugh about it now. I have not yet experienced the humiliation of falling in front of a crowd; however, since I know myself to be a little clumsy, I've already worked out in my mind how I will handle that inevitable moment. If I ever take a tumble in front of a crowd, rather than immediately jumping back on my feet, my plan is to lie there for about three minutes. After all, whenever we witness someone slip, bump into a wall, or unexpectedly get doused with something, human decency tells us to hold our laughter until we're certain the person is not physically hurt. If I lie there long enough, onlookers will be so concerned about my well-being; they will rush to my aid. They will not dare laugh. I will be controlling the crowd. Embarrassing moment saved! Those types of experiences are light-weight, when compared to the most emotionally damaging, embarrassing experience of my life. Admittedly, it was the culmination of a season of bad behaviour and poor decision making on my part. The news of it spread like a virus until it reached my own ears, as I sat in the chair at the hair salon. I was stuck. My hair wasn't even dry yet, so I couldn't even walk out. I couldn't control the crowd. I sat there quietly, amidst the judgment and the laughter, and only released my tears when I got home.

> People may laugh, criticize, and judge us, but they do not have the ability to condemn us.

John 8 tells a story of a woman who was caught in the act of adultery. The leaders brought the woman out into the middle of the community with the intent of shaming her and stoning her to death. Having been exposed to a few people in this manner would have been humiliating to say the least, but to add to her humiliation, her life had become a spectacle and her reputation public record. The woman had no choice but to lie on the ground and await her fate at the hands of her spectators. Thankfully, the woman was brought to the one person who could rescue her. When the leaders presented the woman to Jesus, they asked Him what His opinion was on the matter. According to the old laws, she should have been put to death. Jesus's response was one that would set the precedent for all humanity, as it pertains to how we treat each other in times of misfortune. He said, "He who is without sin among you, let him be the first to throw a stone at her" (John 8:7). One by one, the woman's accusers walked away with the realization that they too had made mistakes, and none were in the position to condemn the woman. After some time, everyone had left and only Jesus remained with the woman. He freed her from her embarrassment, saying, "I do not condemn you either. Go. From now on sin no more" (John 8:11).

Embarrassment comes as a result of our vulnerabilities and weaknesses being exposed. When others become aware of our imperfections, our mistakes, and missteps, that's when we begin to feel ashamed. It happened to Adam and Eve in the garden. After they had sinned, they immediately saw each other's nakedness. Their shame made them anxious to hide themselves from the Lord. We weaken the grip of embarrassment when we make the decision to get up and go on. We can't control the dialogue of others, but we can influence it with our actions. People may laugh, criticize, and judge us, but they do not have the ability to condemn us. When we get up, we are making the declaration that regardless of what has happened in the past, we still have hope for a better future because God gives us a fresh start.

## SUGGESTED READING

Isaiah 50:7 "For the Lord GOD helps Me, Therefore, I am not disgraced; Therefore, I have set My face like flint, And I know that I will not be ashamed."

Jude 24–25 "Now to Him who is able to keep you from stumbling, and to make you stand in the presence of His glory blameless with great joy, to the only God our Savior, through Jesus Christ our Lord, be glory, majesty, dominion and authority, before all time and now and forever. Amen."

# DAY 23

# Darkness

Bedtime is often a time of revelation for our children in our home. Of course, this is also every child's way of avoiding falling asleep. Sometimes, the boys will use that quiet time to run through the events of the day and ask questions about the things that they didn't understand. Other times, just when we think that they are asleep, one or both will begin stating random facts discovered through their daily observations. One night, the youngest discovered that darkness wasn't as scary as others make it out to be. The conversation went something like:

Son: Mommy, did you know that I can see in the dark?

Me: You can?

Son: Yes, I can. When you turn the lights out, it's really dark at first and I can't see anything, but then after I blink a couple times, my eyes start seeing everything again.

Me: That's because your eyes start adjusting to the darkness.

Son: How do they adjust?
Me: That's the way God made our eyes.
Son: But how does it work?
Me: I don't know. You can google it tomorrow. Good
    night.

I won't win any parenting awards for my final response, but it was way past bedtime, and, truthfully, I had no answer. I did follow my own advice, however, by doing a Google search, so that I could give a satisfactory response the next day.

My limited research gave me some very general information. Our ability to see in the dark has something to do with rod and cone cells and a chemical called rhodopsin. I won't pretend to understand it all, but the bottom line is that rhodopsin breaks down into molecules when there is light, and when it is dark, it takes time, but the molecules eventually come together to form rhodopsin again, enabling night vision. If I have already lost you with this explanation, you can only imagine how long my son's attention lasted!

## Darkness ends with the rising of the sun.

Our dark moments can be blinding. Not knowing what the future holds, nor what our next move should be, can be paralyzing to our minds. Hope comes, however, from knowing that, during those moments of blindness, things are slowly coming together in the background to make things clearer. Romans 8:28 says it this way, "And we know that God causes all things to work together for good to those who love God, to those who are called according to His purpose." The other beautiful thing about darkness is that it doesn't last forever. Nighttime ends when morning comes, and darkness ends with the rising of the sun. It is unnerving and uncomfortable, but if we would just be patient, our challenges and our solutions will become clearer to us. Along with the clarity, will come the light from the sunrise, and a new day.

## SUGGESTED READING

John 8:12 "Then Jesus again spoke to them, saying, 'I am the Light of the world; he who follows Me will not walk in the darkness, but will have the Light of life.'"

Isaiah 58:8–9 "Then your light will break out like the dawn, And your recovery will speedily spring forth; And your righteousness will go before you; The glory of the LORD will be your rear guard. Then you will call, and the LORD will answer; You will cry, and He will say, 'Here I am.'"

## DAY 24

# Still Tripping

In his eagerness to get to each destination, one of my sons (I won't say which) has a tendency to misjudge the space he has allotted for footsteps. This lack of accuracy in stepping forward often results in him tripping over his own feet. Alright, I'll just say it and pray that he forgives me for using him as an example; he is a little clumsy. I will also say that this trait is most likely inherited from me. He is also, however, resilient and brilliant with an extraordinary ability to learn from his missteps and improve. He has tripped himself so much that, now, when he falls, rather than lying down and waiting for someone to notice, he will immediately jump back up on his feet and yell, "I'm okay!"

The longer we stay down, the more difficult it becomes to get up.

2 Samuel 11–12 tells the story of King David, who tripped himself up often. Most notably, he had an affair with a married woman; got her pregnant; tried to set her husband up to trick him into believing he was the baby's father; and when that plan failed, had the husband assassinated. As a consequence of David's sins, the Lord told David that the baby would die. The Bible says that David spent days lying on the floor, praying and lamenting before God. People who stood around watching him, no doubt were whispering and forming their own conclusions. After days of fasting and praying for the newborn baby, David got the news that the baby had indeed died. Despite this elaborate fall, David did not stay down. When he finally got word that the child had died, David did the bravest thing that he could do. He got up. When his servants asked him why he was getting up, his response was simply that there was no way he could bring the child back to life. He determined in his heart that there was no use wallowing in self-pity and regret. He could not go back in time to change what happened. Instead, what he could do was move forward and do better. In order to continue to live out his life's purpose and assignment, he needed to get back on his feet and declare that he was okay. The Lord had forgiven him. He had a clean slate. That was not the end of his story.

We have all made some bad decisions. Sometimes those decisions snowball into more bad decisions. Often, we don't realize how badly we've messed up until we start losing the people and things that matter most to us. What we do after that is crucial to our success. Have you ever been sick in bed for more than three days? Whenever you try to get up, your muscles ache and your joints are stiff. In fact, doctors will suggest that you, if you are able, try to get up and walk around for a few minutes each day. The same can be said about our mental ailments. The longer we stay down in our minds, the more difficult it becomes to get up. The truth is, when we do fall in life, staying down only stifles our life's journey.

You may be at the tail end of your fall. Maybe you are still dealing with the consequences of your actions. It's time for you to get back up on your feet now. You can't change what happened, and mourning over your losses will not cause you to recover them. You are not the first, nor the last, to trip over your own feet. You are human, born into sin and shaped in iniquity (Psalm 51:5). The good news is that no matter how many times you fall, the Lord will never withdraw His mercy from you. His loving-kindness is from everlasting to everlasting (Psalm 103:17). After you ask Him to forgive you, go ahead and forgive yourself. Jump back up on your feet and yell, "I'm okay!"

## SUGGESTED READING

Romans 3:23–24 "for all have sinned and fall short of the glory of God, being justified as a gift by His grace through the redemption which is in Christ Jesus;"

2 Corinthians 5:17 "Therefore if anyone is in Christ, he is a new creature; the old things passed away; behold, new things have come."

# DAY 25

# The Big Kick

I've always had a very competitive spirit. Growing up, my older brother and I would make up games just to see who was better. From card games to singing competitions, we were constantly competing against each other. I believe that I passed that characteristic on to my oldest son. He doesn't take well to losing. While my husband takes on the perspective that it's just a game, we hold firm to the thought that it's never just a game! My youngest, however, lands somewhere in between the two extremes. While he loves and appreciates winning the game, he is also just as happy to be playing at all. I learned this about him while watching him play his first house league soccer game. He understood the rules and the object of the game, yet he was most thrilled when he had the biggest kick that spanned half of the field and went out of bounds past the net. He screamed in his most excited outdoor voice, "Did you see how big that kick was?" They may or may not have won the game that day, but for him, the victory wasn't in the win, it was in that awesome kick.

# Celebrate little victories along the way.

In John 6, the Bible tells of a trip that the disciples took across the lake Capernaum. As they were sailing, a rough storm began. In the midst of the storm, they looked out to see Jesus walking on the water toward them. The disciple, Peter, petitioned Him so that he too could walk on the water. In the moments that followed, Peter walked on the water toward Jesus. Those were moments of victory. The story is often told to warn us that when we take our focus off the Lord, we will begin to sink in life's challenging times, during the storms of life. This lesson bears great truth. I would also emphasize another lesson however. Sometimes our victories are not found in controlling the storm but, rather, in those few moments when we are able to walk on the water.

It's natural for us to want to win, to want to be in control of our own outcomes. Sometimes, however, we get so caught up in winning that we forget to enjoy the game. Within the game are small victories. In soccer, it's a great kick; in life, it's being able to pay some bills even if you can't pay them all. It's being able to take public transportation when you can't afford to buy a car. A small victory is when you chase after your dreams, recognizing that you may not attain them right away but, get a little closer every day. Life is a journey. Hope encourages us to celebrate little victories along the way.

## SUGGESTED READING

Romans 12:12 "rejoicing in hope, persevering in tribulation, devoted to prayer."

Psalm 71:14 "But as for me, I will hope continually, And will praise You yet more and more."

# DAY 26

# Time

We have a routine conversation at the end of every school day. The boys are asked two questions: what was the best part of your day? and what was the worst part of your day? Somehow, in the midst of the answers, we can usually gain an understanding of the day's events that we, as parents, are not present for. The responses that we get are often centered around their friends—who made new ones, who was mean, who brought a game to school, which girls chased them, and who told funny jokes. Other times, they talk about goals that they scored in sports or bruises that they acquired from falling on the playground. This type of discussion helps them to understand that every day is constructed with various moments in time. Some moments are joyful, others painful. How we process and respond to each moment reflects our ability to understand time. Time is ever changing, always moving, and it never repeats itself. Every moment in time represents an opportunity for change. Things could get worse, but things could also get better.

# There is still hope for tomorrow.

Jesus came to the earth on a mission to redeem humankind and restore them to a divine relationship with His Father. After His three years of ministry on earth to the poor, sick, and lost, the time came for Him to sacrifice His life on the cross. The night that the soldiers arrested Jesus was filled with a series of events that seemingly got worse with each passing moment. The evening began with a great dinner, wine, and the company of close friends. The evening then began to unravel (or progress, depending on your perspective). Jesus was betrayed by one of His disciples and arrested by soldiers, while His friends scattered. One of His dearest friends subsequently denied having any connection to Him. Jesus was then accused of blasphemy and sentenced to death by crucifixion.

The end of the day for Jesus was drastically different from the beginning. The days that followed seemed to implode with each passing moment. To the onlooker, it would seem that Jesus's life was spiraling out of control; but the truth of the matter is that every moment, good and bad, was a part of God's plan. The good news is that although Jesus died one day, after three days, He rose from the dead and is now alive! Every second of Jesus's life was purposeful, and it led to His ultimate victory over sin and death.

Sometimes when you evaluate your days, they will reveal more failure than success. Just when you think things may be shifting in your favor, you will often feel the retraction of peace and the force of pain. It is during those times that you need to grab a hold of your hope in the Lord. Just as He orchestrated the events of Jesus's life, He has also orchestrated yours. Each moment in time presents a new possibility for change. Each moment of your life, good and bad, is a part of God's plan. Time, with all of its changes, is in God's hands. Even if the last thirty minutes of your day are the worst, there is still hope for tomorrow, and no matter what day one looks like, just like Jesus, you will have a third day.

## SUGGESTED READING

Hebrews 12:1–2 "Therefore, since we have so great a cloud of witnesses surrounding us, let us also lay aside every encumbrance and the sin which so easily entangles us, and let us run with endurance the race that is set before us, fixing our eyes on Jesus, the author and perfecter of faith, who for the joy set before Him endured the cross, despising the shame, and has sat down at the right hand of the throne of God."

Psalm 90:12 "So teach us to number our days, That we may present to You a heart of wisdom."

Ecclesiastes 3:1–4 "There is an appointed time for everything. And there is a time for every event under heaven—

A time to give birth and a time to die;

A time to plant and a time to uproot what is planted.

A time to kill and a time to heal;

A time to tear down and a time to build up.

A time to weep and a time to laugh;

A time to mourn and a time to dance."

# DAY 27

# Loneliness

Some of the loneliest times in my life were times when I was surrounded by a plethora of family, friends, and colleagues. I struggled to understand why I felt so alone when there were people around me who loved me and cared about my well-being. There were people around me who needed me; my survival was important to their survival. We are communal beings. We draw strength from our interactions with other humans. When we are alone, we miss out on that communal strength. I couldn't understand why being around others seemed to weaken rather than strengthen me. At my lowest point, I stopped eating, pulled away from conversations and social media communications, and spent a lot of time not wanting to do anything but cry. I prayed to God for help. I couldn't really explain what I needed, but I figured if anyone knew what I needed, it was Him.

After all, God made me. He knows me better than I know myself.

## He will walk with you as you walk with Him.

Being alone, though similar, is not the same as feeling lonely. You could be in room with fifty other people, but unless those people know you in your most vulnerable state, your truest self, your flaws and idiosyncrasies, and still want to be close to you, you will feel lonely. Loneliness exists in the spaces where you have to always put on your best face, where you have to lead without making mistakes, and where you never feel comfortable letting on that you are uncomfortable. You will experience freedom from loneliness when you are able to connect with someone who you can fully expose your soul to, without fear of judgment. When you have found someone who meets you at the core of who you are, and yet you can trust them with your life, that's when loneliness dissipates.

Jesus hung on the cross for hours before breathing His final breath. He had crowds around Him, some with whom He had close relationship with, others who persecuted Him, unaware that He was their savior. Saturated with the sins of the world, for the first time in His life, Jesus was separated from His Father. He was not alone in His agony, but for those moments, Jesus was lonely. He cried out, "MY GOD, MY GOD, WHY HAVE YOU FORSAKEN ME?" (Mark 15:34) One would think that those moments of solitude would have been the end of Jesus's hope. After all, He was about to die.

Instead, Jesus directed His hope toward what He knew to be certain. God, His Father, loved Him. So that He would fulfill His purpose, Jesus had to remain on the cross. He was determined to sacrifice His life for the redemption of the world. Jesus felt the most forsaken when He was on the brink of accomplishing His mission. Instead of remaining in that forsaken place, He made the decision to place His life in the hands of the Father. He cried out again to the one who knew Him best and who He knew to be in control, "Father, INTO YOUR HANDS I COMMIT MY SPIRIT." (Luke 23:46)

As you go through your days of isolation and loneliness, I urge you to direct your hope towards the Lord. That hope rests on the faith that God is always present. He knows you best and He has chosen never to leave you or forsake you. He has given your life a purpose and a mission; He will walk with you as you walk with Him. When you are on the brink of fulfilling your assignment, the weight of loneliness will increase. Don't give up hope; trust God. Place your life in His hands.

## SUGGESTED READING

Psalm 139:1–10
> O Lord, You have searched me and known me.
> You know when I sit down and when I rise up;
> You understand my thought from afar.
> You scrutinize my path and my lying down,
> And are intimately acquainted with all my ways.
> Even before there is a word on my tongue,
> Behold, O LORD, You know it all.

You have enclosed me behind and before,
And laid Your hand upon me.
Such knowledge is too wonderful for me;
It is too high, I cannot attain to it.
Where can I go from Your Spirit?
Or where can I flee from Your presence?
If I ascend to heaven, You are there;
If I make my bed in Sheol, behold, You are there.
If I take the wings of the dawn,
If I dwell in the remotest part of the sea,
Even there Your hand will lead me,
And Your right hand will lay hold of me.

# DAY 28

# Death

My father-in-law, a two-time cancer survivor, took ill early this year. When the doctors investigated his illness, they discovered that the cancer had returned. It moved very quickly the third time around. Our entire family, our communities, and churches agreed in prayer and cried out to God for healing. The Lord had healed him before; we knew that He was able to do it again. This bout of cancer, however, was different. The doctors weren't able to get a handle on it as they did before. Instead of getting better, his condition declined. We didn't want to let go of our faith, but we began to prepare ourselves for the worst. We packed up the family and made the nineteen-hour drive to spend time with him. Upon our arrival, he expressed his love for all of us and his joy to see us. His next words were, "I've done all that the Lord told me to do. I'm ready to go home now." Those words were piercing to our hearts, but what followed the pain was a sense of peace. There was peace in knowing that my father-in-law's faith rested in the hope that he would see the Lord, and that in His presence, he would finally be healed.

## Hope is a reminder that the Lord will always win.

Some of our favorite scriptures are the ones that reference our victories—scriptures that talk about our healing, others that confirm the power that we have within us. All scripture is true, but it is often difficult to reconcile the Word of God with our disappointments, when things don't go the way that we expect them to go. In his final days, my father-in-law taught me how to do just that. Death did not defeat him. In his death, he is still, more than a conqueror (Romans 8:37). Even in death, he still has resurrection power (Romans 8:11). In death, the Lord is still his healer (Exodus 15:26). His healing may not have come while he was here on earth, but now that he is with the Lord, he is healed. He may not have conquered cancer here on earth, but now he has the victory over it. He may not have resurrected from death yet, but one day, when Jesus returns, my father-in-law will be among the dead who rise first to meet Jesus in the sky (1 Thessalonians 4:16).

We are often sad because we miss my father-in-law's presence, but our hope rests in our belief that we will see him again, and when we do, we will see a victor. Whether you are facing death for yourself or a loved one, maybe you are suffering beyond what you deem as your capacity. Know that your situation does not contradict the Word of God. Hope is a reminder that the Lord will always win.

Whether you see that victory here on earth, or in heaven, it is a sure thing.

## SUGGESTED READING

Revelation 21:1–4 "Then I saw a new heaven and a new earth; for the first heaven and the first earth passed away, and there is no longer any sea. And I saw the holy city, new Jerusalem, coming down out of heaven from God, made ready as a bride adorned for her husband. And I heard a loud voice from the throne, saying, 'Behold, the tabernacle of God is among men, and He will dwell among them, and they shall be His people, and God Himself will be among them, and He will wipe away every tear from their eyes; and there will no longer be any death; there will no longer be any mourning, or crying, or pain; the first things have passed away.'"

1 Corinthians 15:54–55 "But when this perishable will have put on the imperishable, and this mortal will have put on immortality, then will come about the saying that is written, 'DEATH IS SWALLOWED UP in victory. O DEATH, WHERE IS YOUR VICTORY? O DEATH, WHERE IS YOUR STING?'"

## DAY 29

# The Raccoon

It was a cold and quiet night at home with the family. That's the way most thrillers start. I had just put the children to bed and had begun to straighten up the house. I was emptying the garbage bin in the kitchen and because garbage pickup was not the next day, I had to put the bag in the giant bin in our backyard. This was usually a chore that my husband took on but he was out for the evening so I decided to brave it myself. After all, how hard could it be to open the door, walk down the steps, open the bin and drop a bag in there? Well, I walked toward the door, put my hand on the doorknob and before I could turn the knob, I looked up to see a giant raccoon standing on the steps, on its hind feet, staring at me through the glass. I don't know if it was standing there in anticipation of our garbage or if it was waiting to attack me, but I was not about to find out. I let out a squeal loud enough to wake the children, but thankfully they did not come downstairs. The raccoon didn't budge. I slowly started to back away as we stared each other down. When I backed into the kitchen counter, I grabbed my cell phone and walked forward again to the door. I turned on the flash and took a picture of what I now considered a stalker. Not even the bright light from the flash made him move. He just kept looking at me. I texted the picture to my husband, hoping that he would tell me what to do. His reply was, "Just keep the door closed; he can't get to you." Those words were simple but reassuring. The raccoon could see me through the glass, he could intimidate me with his posture, but he could not get to me. I eventually turned out the lights in the house and after about two or three more minutes, he finally left. Or maybe he was just hiding. I don't know because I didn't go into our backyard for months after that.

# You will be safe.

The Book of Job notes that Job was an upright man whose life pleased God. He was blessed with a large family, numerous possessions, and great wealth. Satan tried to challenge God by saying that the only reason Job was faithful to Him was because of all that God had blessed him with, suggesting that if he didn't have those things, Job would turn his back on God. God gave Satan permission to test Job by interfering with his life, his family, and his possessions; the only thing that Satan was not able to do was take Job's life. Job's trials were extensive. He lost his family, his health, his possessions, and his friends. Though life was excruciatingly painful and difficult for him, Job never cursed God. His story ends with God blessing Job with a double portion of everything that he had lost, and the Bible tells us that his latter days were greater than all he had gone through in the past.

Your biggest fears may be staring you in the face right now. Maybe you've lost some people or things that you thought you would have forever. Perhaps you are being attacked in a way that feels unnerving. The situation that you find yourself in could very well be a test of your ability to hold on to your convictions and your hope. Do not give your fears an open door to your mind. As long as that door is closed, they cannot get to you. Hope says that God is always in control and you will be safe.

## SUGGESTED READING

Romans 8:31 "What then shall we say to these things? If God is for us, who is against us?"

Isaiah 54:17 "No weapon that is formed against you will prosper; And every tongue that accuses you in judgment you will condemn. This is the heritage of the servants of the LORD, And their vindication is from Me," declares the LORD."

Psalm 121

I will lift up my eyes to the mountains;
From where shall my help come?
My help comes from the LORD,
Who made heaven and earth.
He will not allow your foot to slip;
He who keeps you will not slumber.
Behold, He who keeps Israel
Will neither slumber nor sleep.
The LORD is your keeper;
The LORD is your shade on your right hand.
The sun will not smite you by day,

Nor the moon by night.
The LORD will protect you from all evil;
He will keep your soul.
The LORD will guard your going out and your
     coming in
From this time forth and forever.

## DAY 30

# Abandoned Cart

I have a few websites that I shop from regularly, but every now and then, I will see an ad pop up on my computer luring me to shop on a new site. I clicked on a random ad for furniture one day. It led me to a 60 percent off sale on some very beautiful contemporary items. I added four items to my shopping cart before heading to the checkout. After entering my personal information, I was directed to the page where I was supposed to enter my payment information. It was at that moment that I changed my mind. I forgot to mention, along with my other issues, I often suffer from buyer's remorse. I don't like to spend money, and when I do, I usually regret it deeply. Thankfully, I have a husband that will talk me into keeping whatever I've purchased. He brings balance to my life in so many ways. God really knew what He was doing when He put us together. That particular time however, he wasn't around, so I just abandoned the cart. One year later, I came across an ad for some very cool furniture on sale for 40 percent off. I clicked on the link and perused the website for a short while. Interestingly, I noticed in the top right corner of the screen that there were four items in my shopping cart. I clicked on the cart, certain that it was a mistake, only to discover the items that I had selected one year before. I didn't even realize that I was visiting the same online store yet, there it was, my abandoned shopping cart. Everything in the cart was still appealing to me; the only difference was that the 60 percent off sale had long since ended and everything was now 40 percent off instead.

## God doesn't change His mind about us.

God is much like that online store. When we walk away from Him, He doesn't discard everything that He has set aside for us. Instead, He holds on to all of that goodness until we return to Him. During His final meal with His disciples, Jesus told Peter that before the night was out, he would deny Him three times. Peter was adamant that this would never happen. Nevertheless, after Jesus was arrested, Peter was spotted by people who were certain that he was one of Jesus's friends. When asked about it, Peter denied having any association with Jesus. Though Jesus was not standing next to him at the time, when Peter denied Christ, he was, in a sense, abandoning Him. Jesus had big plans for Peter. He was supposed to be the one to lead the way in establishing churches, yet he turned his back on Jesus. Thankfully, Peter was given another chance at fulfilling his purpose. After Jesus's death, burial, resurrection, and ascension to heaven, Peter preached his first public sermon, and thousands of people responded by becoming followers of Christ. The church had begun.

Peter abandoned his cart. The wonderful thing about the divine purpose of God is that He already knows that we will walk away before we walk away. God doesn't change His mind about us because of the poor decisions that we make. It is incumbent upon us, however, to return to the Lord and to His plans for our lives. Hope says that it's not too late. As long as you have breath in your body, you can decide to revisit that place, and that relationship with the Lord, that you abandoned and receive all that God has for you.

## SUGGESTED READING

Proverbs 13:12 "Hope deferred makes the heart sick, But desire fulfilled is a tree of life."

Philippians 1:6 "For I am confident of this very thing, that He who began a good work in you will perfect it until the day of Christ Jesus."

2 Corinthians 1:20 "For as many as are the promises of God, in Him they are yes; therefore also through Him is our Amen to the glory of God through us."

# DAY 31

# God

I was having one of those days. To be quite honest, it was one of quite a few days. For several months, I felt myself becoming numb to life. I had no answer for my husband, who noticed and questioned me. I could barely understand it myself. I loved the Lord. I trusted Him. I relied on the joy of my salvation for my strength, yet there I was in a dark place. Even in the middle of writing a book about hope, my own determination was being challenged. The stress that I thought I had mastered was taking its toll on me physically and emotionally. The responsibilities that I had become a professional at juggling, felt like heavy weights. Every little thing made me angry, sad, or both. I was sinking into an impermissible depression. It was impermissible because I spent so much of my life dedicated to helping others get out of the place that I had now found myself in. I prayed, cried, and often shut down emotionally in private, but in public, I was able to put a smile on my face and an encouraging word in my mouth for anyone else who needed it. The peak of these moments was hit one evening when I blew up on my husband. He was totally undeserving of my verbal attack, and I knew it immediately, but I didn't have the capacity to come down from the disastrous height of emotion. I whispered a quiet prayer to the Lord, "Please help me get out of this state." Right away, I felt the nudge from His spirit, telling me to go for a walk.

I stopped at a nearby park and took a seat on the bench. It was getting dark, so I tried to be aware of my surroundings. I noticed a man drive up, get out of his car, and walk in my direction. He stood not too far away from me with his back turned. He lifted his cell phone and took a picture of one of the most beautiful sunsets that I had ever seen. I was so consumed with my own feelings that I didn't notice it. I would have missed it completely, had this man not drawn it to my attention. He paused and stared at the sky for about twenty seconds before turning to walk back to his vehicle. I don't know if he was aware of me observing him, but he stopped in front of me and asked my name. I answered him and asked him his name. After he stated his name, he shrugged his shoulders. I wondered if he thought that his name was strange, or that it lacked importance. I didn't understand why he shrugged. I told the gentleman that I thought he had taken a picture of a beautiful sunset. He agreed. He then pointed to me and said, "You will be healthy and wealthy for the rest of your life." I was so taken back by his statement that I didn't even return words of affirmation to him. I just said thank you, as he turned to walk away. He got back into his car and drove away. I don't know if we will ever cross paths again. I don't know if he was an angel or just a neighbor, but I believe that the Lord divinely ordained that moment to remind me to hold on to my hope; it is not in vain. My hope reminds me that regardless of what I am experiencing, the Lord will keep my spiritual health and spiritual wealth intact. My hope says that the Lord will keep me in perfect peace when I keep my mind on Him and trust Him (Isaiah 26:3).

## The beauty of God supersedes the ugliness of your circumstances.

Acts 6–7 tells us about the apostle Stephen. The Bible says that he went about preaching the Gospel of Jesus Christ and performing signs and wonders. While there were many who were receptive and converted to Christianity, there were several groups that became angry and determined to stop him. They accused him of blasphemy and took him before the council to be judged. After stating his case before the council, the elders became angrier and chased him out of the city. Stephen was then stoned to death. What amazes me about Stephen, the martyr, is while he was surrounded by negative words and attacks, the Bible says that Stephen was filled with the Holy Spirit, and instead of focusing on all that was going wrong, he looked only to heaven and saw the glory of God. In the midst of his trouble, Stephen declared for all of the people to hear, "Behold I see the heavens opened up and the Son of Man standing at the right hand of God" (Acts 7:56). In the midst of chaos, Stephen experienced a time of beauty and tranquility by fixing his focus on the all-powerful and loving God. Romans 8:34

says that Jesus is at the right hand of the father, interceding for us. Stephen caught a glimpse of that very promise.

Your present situation may be chaotic, burdensome, and often overwhelming, but rest assured that Jesus is mediating for you. Sometimes we get so overwhelmed with the weight of life that we fail to notice the beauty of it. The beauty rests in the knowledge that Jesus is with us. If we pause long enough, we will see Him, not only in the sunrise but also in the sunset. We see Him in the rainbow after the storm. We see Him in the vastness of unaltered land that others deem to be barren. Hope says that the beauty of God supersedes the ugliness of your circumstances.

## SUGGESTED READING

Psalm 119:114 "You are my hiding place and my shield; I wait for Your word."

Psalm 27:4 "One thing I have asked from the LORD, that I shall seek: That I may dwell in the house of the LORD all the days of my life, To behold the beauty of the LORD And to meditate in His temple."

# FINAL THOUGHT

The mere existence of even a small amount of hope has already crushed some portion of doubt and awakened a possibility.

Our oldest son joined the wrestling team at school. I've learned that the sport is not about the competitors hurting each other; it's more about using special moves and techniques that help them to pin down their opponent or help them to escape the grasp of their opponent. One of the strategies to avoid being pinned down is to do whatever they can to stay on their feet.

We were watching one of his matches, and while he started off strong, at one point, he lost his footing. It was enough of a slip up for his opponent to get him down into a weak position. In those next few seconds, as he struggled to push back and fought to turn over, we could hear a voice from the sidelines, one of his teammates yelling, "Stand up, Elijah! Stand up, Elijah! Come on, Elijah. You've got to stand up!" After he yelled it the third or fourth time, Elijah caught on to the instruction. We watched his demeanor change and his confidence rise. Any thought of losing seemed to diminish, as he managed to find his footing and stand up on his feet. Once he was standing, it was difficult for his opponent to get him down again, and he went on to win the match.

So much of our success is determined by our determination to stand up. Doubt, however, makes standing up hard to do. Doubt is the enemy of hope. The two cannot consume the same space. The mere existence of even a small amount of hope has already crushed some portion of doubt and awakened a possibility. Hope says that whatever the circumstance, change is possible. We all experience moments of doubt. Doubt weighs us down. It makes us to want to quit. We doubt our ability to bounce back. We doubt that we will ever succeed. We doubt our own worth. Doubt is a seed of hopelessness. We are always, however, presented with a choice. We can reside in a state of hopelessness or we can fill our minds with hope. It helps to have someone cheering you on from the sidelines, someone reminding you to stand and keep standing. My prayer is that you have heard those cheers echoing from my heart, as you've read these pages. I am rooting for you. May your pockets be emptied of despair, and filled with hope, that you will carry with you throughout your life, as you go forward.

## SUGGESTED READING

Philippians 4:6–7 "Be anxious for nothing but in everything by prayer and supplication with thanksgiving let your requests be made known to God. And the peace of God, which surpasses all comprehension, will guard your hearts and your minds in Christ Jesus."

Psalm 33:20–22 "Our soul waits for the LORD; He is our help and our shield. For our heart rejoices in Him, Because we trust in His holy name. Let Your lovingkindness, O LORD, be upon us, According as we have hoped in You."

# Prayer

Lord, thank you for being a God that I can trust. You never fail. Please help me to have faith in you when doubts arise in my mind. I know that you love me and care about me. I believe that you are working on my behalf. I believe that you can fix anything and change everything. I place all of my hope in you. In Jesus' name I pray. Amen.

# ABOUT THE AUTHOR

Ayesha O. Daniels is a wife, mother, and public speaker. She is passionate about motivating people of all demographics to live their best lives. She uses the Bible, along with her life experiences, to encourage others to pursue their God-given purposes despite the many challenges they may face. As a published songwriter, and now, a published author, she creates works that build the esteem and character of her audience.

With a BA, Religious Studies and MA, Discipleship Ministries, Ayesha specifically thrives on helping women to see their value and significance in impacting an ever-changing world. She firmly believes that transparency in sharing our stories with each other helps to maintain our connectivity and accountability. Ayesha and her husband, Bobby, serve at their local church as pastors and relationship mentors, helping husbands and wives to maintain and fight for healthy marriages.

Ayesha resides in the Greater Toronto Area, Canada, with her husband, Bobby, and two sons, Elijah and Aaron. She loves family time, reading, movies, and musical theater.

CPSIA information can be obtained
at www.ICGtesting.com
Printed in the USA
BVHW070453111122
651712BV00006B/162